This journal belongs to:

_____

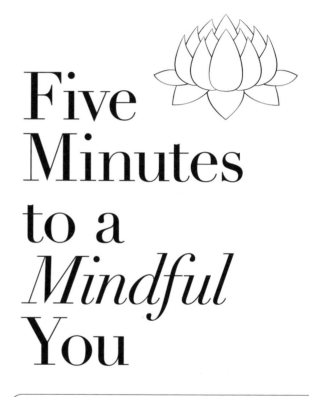

Five Minutes to a *Mindful* You

A GUIDED JOURNAL FOR SELF-REFLECTION

An Hachette UK Company
www.hachette.co.uk

First published in Great Britain in 2018 by Aster, an imprint of
Octopus Publishing Group Ltd
Carmelite House
50 Victoria Embankment
London EC4Y 0DZ
www.octopusbooks.co.uk
www.octopusbooksusa.com

Distributed in the US by
Hachette Book Group
1290 Avenue of the Americas
4th and 5th Floors
New York, NY 10104

Distributed in Canada by
Canadian Manda Group
664 Annette St.
Toronto, Ontario, Canada M6S 2C8

ISBN 978 1 91202 397 4

A CIP catalogue record for this book is available from the British Library.

Printed and bound in China

10 9 8 7 6 5 4 3 2 1

CONTENTS

INTRODUCTION FIVE MINUTES JUST FOR YOU

Writing mindfully for just a few minutes each day is a wonderful practice for bringing you into the present moment. It encourages you to notice your own presence and how you are feeling right now in your body and mind. And it encourages you to notice and be engaged with the richness of life in all its detail – the pure joy and the pure heartache, it is all part of our experience of life.

The process of writing things down is something that allows you to release emotions or thoughts that have become stuck or held too tightly, from the emotional baggage of the day to deeper-rooted limiting beliefs and thought patterns.

It's amazing how many things that you are grateful for can be expressed on paper in five minutes – even in just one minute. And researchers have found that writing about what you are grateful for, rather than simply thinking about these things, is linked to better sleep, lower anxiety levels and improved mood.

Similarly, it takes only a few moments to express on paper all the resources that you carry with you each day, from your sense of humour to the things you know help to relax or nourish you.

And because writing and other creative activities put your mind into a meditative or "theta" brainwave state, journaling can even help to rewire your brain. A calmer mind copes more easily with stressful situations and makes decisions more effectively. You are able to spot your habits and patterns, jot them down and, with that simple act of awareness, take steps toward loosening their control over your thoughts and behaviour.

A DIFFERENT KIND OF DAY

Give yourself just five minutes and you may discover that you experience a different kind of day. If you try a mindfulness practice such as journaling first thing in the morning, studies show that you are more likely to report having had a good day at the end of it, even when the usual challenges come your way. Putting your mind into a calm state is helpful, therefore, in overwriting the usual tendency to dwell more on negative thoughts than on positive ones.

This journal is designed to offer prompts and exercises that bring you into a state of awareness from which to write a few lines or a few words, that develop your self-awareness so that you can connect more freely with your inner, present self, with others, with the world around you and with your experience of life.

As you begin to journal, be aware of your natural rhythm and which times of the day feel best for you to develop this mindful practice. And it is useful to think of this as a practice, which will evolve and deepen through your intention and commitment to it.

WHAT MAKES JOURNALING "MINDFUL"?

Journaling is an opportunity for self-inquiry and exploration. It is just you, your thoughts and feelings and a notebook. There is so much potential in this simplicity. You are giving yourself permission to be present with yourself, open up your senses and listen to the whispers from within.

Writing something down enables it to be processed. Old emotions are given acknowledgment and can then be released to make room for new manifestations or dreams. Writing also sharpens your powers of observation, so that you can live each day with increased awareness of your connections with others and the world around you. And when you notice the details of life, it is like a flower that blossoms.

"*Nature may have done something, but I am sure it must be essentially assisted by the practice of keeping a journal.*"

JANE AUSTEN

MINDFULNESS ISN'T ALL ABOUT HAPPINESS

Mindfulness will stumble across happiness by chance and will heighten your awareness of when you experience happiness, but it will also bring your attention to so much more. Mindfulness is permission to truly experience what you are feeling, without attachment to those feelings. One morning or evening, as you write, you might experience sadness or frustration or longing. The key with any mindful practice is to allow yourself to notice, experience and investigate thoughts or emotions that ask for your attention, without becoming those thoughts or emotions.

You are not your thoughts. Thoughts come into the mind and are often very powerful and tempting to claim as a set belief – I am shy, I don't cry – but nothing is set, nothing is permanent. Notice it, feel it, but don't take ownership.

In writing difficult or painful thoughts and emotions down, you are taking a step toward truly accepting what is. When we are in acceptance, we are no longer gripped by such thoughts or emotions. This is not to say that you suddenly become happy in any painful situation or that you don't take steps to improve a situation, but you are no longer gripped by the things that you can't control, and you can begin to focus on the steps you can take.

TAKING NOTICE

At the heart of any mindful practice is awareness – the art of paying attention. We have so many distractions throughout the day that it can be very helpful to deliberately and consciously spend a few minutes taking notice. You might simply notice the thoughts running around your mind, which in itself loosens their intensity, or stop to notice the details in your immediate surroundings.

BREATHE

"For breath is life, and if you breathe well you will live long on earth."

SANSKRIT PROVERB

Mindfulness starts with the breath. Before you begin to write, take a few deep, relaxed breaths and bring your attention gently to your inhale and then your exhale. Simply "be" in this moment; there is no need to do anything but breathe fully into every part of your body. Give yourself these moments of spaciousness and openness, which are a wonderful invitation to self-reflection and exploration.

INTO THE
PRESENT MOMENT

The past is behind you, the future lies ahead and life is truly experienced in the present moment. Every sunrise and sunset reminds us that nothing stays exactly the same, but each of these moments is precious, the beginning or end of a new day. When you begin to journal, writing down your thoughts and emotions and things that you simply notice, you are bringing your awareness more fully into the present and into your experience of life.

*"Don't let yesterday take up
too much of today."*

NATIVE AMERICAN PROVERB

LIFE IS IN THE DETAIL

Find an object that is particularly beautiful to you.

Describe it in great detail.

What is it about the object that you find beautiful?

Describe your own feelings in response to noticing the object's beauty and detail.

DOING NOTHING

Once in a while, cherish the moment by simply *being*, not *doing*.

Sit on a bench.

Stare out of the window.

Wander along.

With this frame of mind, make a few jottings, notes that needn't lead anywhere in particular. How does it feel to just *be* in this moment? What do you notice?

MONO NO AWARE

"Mono no aware" is a phrase linked to the Japanese aesthetics of impermanence, the melancholic beauty in the fact that nothing is permanent in life. The concept of impermanence is often linked to nature, where the seasons show us so poignantly and beautifully that nothing remains the same.

It is often symbolized by the cherry blossoms that come each spring in Japan for such a short time, and which are so stunningly beautiful – perhaps more so for the fact that their time is so fleeting.

Explore the concept of impermanence in your own life. Can you detect its beauty, even in the sadness?

GOKÖTTA

"The thrushes sing as the sun is going,
And the finches whistle in ones and pairs,
And as it gets dark loud nightingales
In bushes
Pipe, as they can when April wears,
As if all Time were theirs."

THOMAS HARDY, *PROUD SONGSTERS*

"Gokötta" is a Swedish term that literally means to get up
early in the morning in order to listen to the birds sing.
There is something so life-affirming about the dawn chorus.

What would you be happy to get up early for in your life?

ATTENTION

A candle is often used to focus the mind in meditation. Just a small flame can calm the multitude of random thoughts that whizz around our minds like a pinball machine.

Mindful writing can offer the same degree of calm focus. Simply pick one question or thought or idea and describe it in all its detail – everything that you notice about it. When you find yourself wandering from the topic, gently bring yourself back to explore it again, looking into every corner.

Examples of such thoughts might be:
A dream you had
A dream you wish to have
An ambition not yet embarked upon
A relationship that fills, or filled, you with joy

HOW YOU FEEL

How often do you reply "Fine" to the question
"How are you?", without even thinking about it?

The following exercises are to help you really get
in touch with how you feel, from the way your body
feels, to knowing your boundaries and allowing
your vulnerability to be acknowledged. Writing
mindfully is a practice that can help you develop
presence – and an awareness of presence, both
in yourself and in others or in your surroundings.
When you are present, you are fully alive to
everything that life has to offer.

BODY SCAN

You may wish to write a few notes after this exercise and, as you practise it, whether daily or weekly, your experience may change over time.

To do this mindful exercise, you need a chair and a quiet space where you won't be distracted by people coming into it. Noises beyond the space are natural and are part of the exercise.

Read through the exercise and then try it, as it's best to do it with your eyes closed.

Sit with your back comfortably straight against the chair and with your feet flat on the ground.

Close your eyes and breathe normally, bringing your attention to your breath.

Gradually bring your attention to the crown of your head and just sense if there is "presence" here. Try not to "look" with your mind, but feel this part of your body and whether there is any energy or sensation there.

Now scan each part of your body, again simply bringing an awareness rather than looking. How does your right hand feel versus your left? Can you detect a slightly different level of presence?

Are there areas where you can't really detect any presence? Notice these areas; there is no need to try and change anything or do anything.

When you have scanned your whole body, gently bring your focus back to the breath, bring your awareness into the room where you are sitting and, when you are ready, open your eyes.

AWARENESS
OF WHAT IS

With so many distractions in our modern lives and in our minds, it is not always easy to access a state of awareness. You might spend much of the day on autopilot, walking the same way to work, buying the same type of coffee from the same shop, so that when you take even a few minutes to focus yourself consciously on your state of awareness – even if that means simply noticing how unaware you have been – you might be surprised at the richness of that experience. Take a few moments to settle with yourself and your immediate environment.

Take a few deep, easy breaths and feel free to close your eyes for a few moments to get in touch with a sense of awareness, a sense of your presence and the energy within and around you.

Write these words at the top of the page opposite and then see what happens:

"Right now, in this moment, I am aware that..."

WHAT IS THE QUESTION ARISING TODAY?

Sometimes it feels as though we are looking for answers when we don't even know what the questions are. There is so much going on, it is difficult to know if there is an area of life, or ourselves, that is asking to be explored.

An excellent journal practice is to find a quiet space, allow yourself to settle and ask yourself, "What is the question that wishes to be asked today?"

You may not always have an answer, and that is as it should be; simply write whatever comes in response to the question.

WHAT TOUCHES YOUR SOUL?

Where is the sense of magic in your life? What helps you come into awareness of your own self, awareness of others and awareness of your environment?

If we are to connect with ourselves and how we feel, so that we may then connect fully with those around us, it is a good idea to notice those things that seem to help us feel aware.

It might be those moments when the natural world takes your breath away, or when you stop to catch the scent of a flower. Perhaps it is the kindness of a stranger, a human touch, the sound of a choir.

Describe these moments and you might find they
show up in your life even more.

_____

_____

_____

_____

_____

_____

_____

_____

_____

_____

_____

_____

_____

_____

_____

_____

_____

_____

WHAT WOULD YOUR HEART SAY?

We live in a mind-driven society, and so it isn't always very easy to listen deeply to what your heart is saying. This is where journaling can be so helpful, especially when you allow yourself to write in a stream of consciousness, not worrying about forming specific sentences, not knowing where it might go.

Take a moment to settle and sit quietly, breathing naturally.

Imagine breathing into your heart space. Do this for a few deep, gentle breaths. Breathe in through the nose and breathe out through your mouth, letting go of any tension with your out-breath.

What would your heart say?

Ask yourself the question and simply write – anything at all, it is all good.

WHEN ARE YOU COMFORTABLE IN YOUR SKIN?

"Wherever my travels may lead, paradise is where I am."

VOLTAIRE

Describe a typical situation in your life when you feel comfortable and content. You feel good in yourself, at ease and relaxed. Perhaps you are outside in nature, curled up with a book or chatting with friends.

Such times as these are a great resource to you, and by writing them down, you are more likely to bring more of these situations into your life and less likely to take them for granted. When you are feeling as though your emotional resources are getting low, you can draw on these situations and help yourself to recharge.

WHERE ARE YOUR BOUNDARIES?

As you deepen your sense of self through mindful reflection, you can begin to sense where your boundaries with others are, both physical and emotional, personal and professional.

Boundaries are essential, but sometimes it can feel extremely difficult to know where best to set them. We want to please others, but know deep down that if we allow our boundaries to be trodden over, it doesn't really work for anyone in the situation as we are not valued or fully respected by the other or, even more importantly, by ourselves.

Conversely, if our boundaries are too firm and immovable, then all the spontaneity goes out of life and, by holding on too tightly to our sense of control, we limit ourselves and our capacity for connecting with others.

Reflect on the idea of boundaries and what they mean to you; as you write, consider where you need to be firmer or looser.

WHERE DO YOU FEEL STRONG?

It is a human tendency to focus on where we we wish to improve, often ignoring the positive aspects of ourselves. Imagine a tree, hundreds of years old, with an amazing root system and a strong, yet flexible trunk with limbs that sway in the wind without breaking.

Where is the energy in your body and in your sense of self, right now? Is the flame burning strongly, or do you need to tend the fire and give attention to any of these places or aspects of yourself?

Where is your greatest potential that lies within?

THE SHADOWS

"There can be no transforming of darkness into light… without emotion."

CARL JUNG

It is often thought that mindfulness is only concerned with light, that if we practise mindfulness then we will feel good, or at least better. However, being mindful – and in particular practising mindful writing – gives us an opportunity to explore the shadows in ourselves and in our lives, as well as the light.

You might think: what good will come from going into the shadows? Why cause ourselves more pain and suffering? But it is acknowledging the darkness that creates the possibility for transformation.

When you are in the right frame of mind to do so, when you are feeling calm, gently allow yourself to explore and describe a part of yourself, or your life, that is in the shadows.

WHERE DOES IT HURT?

Writing gives you the space to feel into the places that hurt. This is not the same as becoming attached to the pain; instead try to imagine yourself as the watcher or observer, so that you can acknowledge the pain without becoming consumed by it. Describe where it hurts – this might be a physical pain or an emotional hurt. Perhaps there is an old hurt that wishes to be let go of now.

Try to put a colour on it.

Is it very specific or does it have edges that are difficult to define?

If the pain could say something, what would it say?

USING YOUR SENSES

As you develop your journaling practice, you can begin to bring in all your senses. You might write about a particularly delicious meal or the scent of a flower or a piece of music you listened to. Writing down the experiences of your senses will continue to heighten your awareness of the rich details of everyday life and remind you of all those sensory moments that bring joy or wake you up.

A CUP OF TEA

When camping in the outdoors you are reminded of the wonder of that first morning cup of tea – waiting for the water to boil over the stove or fire, warming your hands over the cup and watching the steam rise as the sun begins to peek over the horizon.

Making a cup of tea before heading out to work might not have the same romantic symbolism, but taking a few moments to sit quietly with a cup of tea or coffee early in the morning creates a sense of stillness that will remain with you through the ups and downs of the day.

Jot down your early-morning thoughts and feelings as you savour
this first cup of the day. Giving thanks to the water that nourishes
you also opens the tap on your own sense of gratitude in your life,
even for the very small things, like a cup of tea.

_____

_____

_____

_____

_____

_____

_____

_____

_____

_____

_____

_____

_____

_____

_____

_____

TASTE

With all the "busyness" of life, taste is often relegated below other senses, even when we are eating. We rarely, if ever, focus entirely on the sensory stimulation of eating. We might be talking at the same time, reading, working, watching television or surfing social media. We might not even know what to do with ourselves without those other distractions – it would feel strange just to eat.

This is a practice that your digestion will thank you for, as studies has shown that the absorption of nutrients is increased when you eat mindfully. And food is a wonderful way to bring us into a place of sensory awareness, which in turn helps us to be more aware of the details of life in general.

The simple act of inwardly saying thank you before you eat will bring your awareness to the food on your plate and to each mouthful. How does the food taste? Is it salty or sweet, does it have heat or is it cooling, like a cucumber?

How can you bring eating mindfully into your daily life?

TOUCH

The human nervous system finds touch very nourishing and balancing, and yet in our modern lives we might go through the day without engaging very much with this sense. Think about the phrase to be "in touch", meaning to be connected with oneself, with one's environment or with others.

Keep a lookout for interesting textures or materials. Even as you open a door, connect with the moment that you take hold of the handle and sense the weight of the door.

To practise becoming more aware of your senses, you can choose an interesting object near you that calls out to your sense of touch. Take it in your hands and describe the object purely through the way it feels to touch it; is it cool or warm, rough or smooth? Where are its imperfections, those tiny things that make it unique?

Or perhaps you might take off your shoes and describe how it feels to walk barefoot on the cool grass, or notice the sensations on your skin as you sit by the ocean, the salty breeze and the warmth of the sun as it comes out from behind a cloud.

> *"In rivers, the water that you touch is the last of what has passed and the first of that which comes; so with present time."*
>
> **LEONARDO DA VINCI**

SOUND

There is a wonderful practice that is growing in popularity, called "sound bathing". Singing bowls and other sound vessels are used as a means of meditation in which sounds are absorbed by the body and mind. Even the sound of a small prayer bell is a powerful way to focus the mind.

In today's busy world, we are often trying to block out sound with earphones, but when you allow yourself to absorb the sounds around you, you may find there are fascinating details that heighten your sense of presence. Sound is, after all, vibration, and so your body constantly resonates with the sounds around you. If you can pay attention to the sensation of listening with your whole body, you become truly aware.

Today, spend a few minutes just listening and absorbing the sounds around you. After you have finished, write down everything that you noticed.

SMELL

University researchers discovered that smelling rosemary might improve your memory. And it is fascinating how specific aromas, such as freshly cut grass, instantly transport our minds to places where our memories have a strong association with that particular smell. The age-old adage "Stop and smell the roses" is a perfect illustration of the connection between our senses and our awareness of being in the present moment. Whatever is happening in your day, pausing for just a few seconds to breathe in the scent of a flower will immediately bring you back to your senses, back into your body and mind in the here and now.

Find a fresh herb and pick a sprig, scrunching up the leaves with your fingers.

Close your eyes and bring the herb, in your hand, up to your nose so that you can inhale deeply and smell the oils released by the herb.

What are the characteristics of the scent? Is it fresh or musky, delicate or strong? Does it bring any memories with it?

Focus on your breath and the aroma entering your body. How does this aroma make you feel?

SAY WHAT YOU SEE

"Vision is the art of seeing what is invisible to others."

JONATHAN SWIFT

Be open and willing to be present in the moment and to say whatever
you see, even if you begin this practice within the privacy of these
pages. Take your time when looking, breathe and ask yourself if you
are seeing without judgment, with open curiosity.

You might observe something physical in your immediate environment
or you might see an idea in its infancy – or, indeed, your own confusion.

Now, say what you see.

SIXTH SENSE

As your awareness of the present moment grows, and with it your awareness of your sense of self and others, you may find that you become more in tune with what might be called your "sixth sense". This your "inner knowing"; you might describe it as your gut instinct, intuition or wisdom.

If you can sense right now where this place of inner knowing resides in your body, describe where that is and how it feels. Give it a colour perhaps or a symbol, such as a candle flame or a precious crystal. You carry this sixth sense with you at all times, just as you have your sense of touch or taste, but it often becomes faint over time. You can use the symbol as a reminder or talisman.

Can you think of a time when you paid attention to your sixth sense and this helped you out, or helped others? Or even a time when you dismissed it and regretted that choice later on? Feel that experience of intuition or instinct.

Trust yourself.

"When you reach the end of what you should know, you will be at the beginning of what you should sense."

KAHLIL GIBRAN, *SAND AND FOAM*

REFLECTION & CONNECTION

Developing a reflective practice through mindful journaling is helpful for deepening your understanding of yourself and others. It encourages you to acknowledge all aspects of yourself, even those that initially feel less attractive or appealing than others, so that you can bring your whole self into your life and your relationships. This allows for deeper connections that are nourishing to the mind, body and soul.

WHERE DO YOU COME FROM?

There is a misconception that the practice of mindfulness means never to consider the past or the future, but only the present. But when you bring your awareness into the present you are then able to reflect on your life and the journey so far with clarity. You can truly see where you have come from and where you are going, while being present in this moment.

Take your time to bring your awareness to your breath and the sensations in your body. As you breathe out, let yourself sigh audibly as you release any tension or tightness – take this time to be present to yourself.

Now, consider the question of where you come from. There are no right or wrong answers, simply write whatever comes up.

WHY ARE YOU HERE?

Knowing what your purpose in life is can be one of the most difficult questions to answer, and if you struggle to feel clarity around this question, then mindful journaling can help you get to the heart of the matter.

The answer might not be summed up in a pithy sentence, but threads of the answer lie throughout this journal: in the things and people that make you feel connected, and the places where you feel awake and energized and your inner knowing comes to the fore more often.

You may come back to this question at many times in your life, or you might have a very strong and clear sense of purpose. But if at first you don't feel confident that you know the answer, use the prompts to explore and ask these questions:

What are you doing when you feel most connected?

What, or who, are you completely inspired by?

What are you good at and also enjoy?

WHAT ARE YOU AFRAID OF?

Fear has an essential part to play at certain moments in our lives. Fear tells us to run away from danger or go for help. It is a warning signal that we are close to our physical limits.

However, just as we learn to keep a safe distance from the edge in the physical world, so we learn to stay clear of the metaphorical edge, and fear can become attached to the idea of taking risks in our work or in our relationships, because "risks" signal danger.

Fear can stop us from growing or expanding to our full potential; the fear of failure is strong for many, and yet every successful person has a list of failures they can describe, along with the invaluable lessons they learned from those failures.

In this safe space, explore what you are afraid of and take your time to observe and acknowledge these fears.

"What you are afraid to do is a clear indication of the next thing you need to do."

RALPH WALDO EMERSON

WHAT DOES HAPPINESS FEEL LIKE TO YOU?

*"Ever since happiness heard your name,
it has been running through the streets
trying to find you."*

HAFIZ

Happiness is in your essence, but it isn't something you can fix into being a permanent state. Its very nature is flowing and changing, like a river. What you can do is become increasingly aware of the moments when happiness is there, from experiences of joy to those deeper, quieter moments of utter contentment.

What does happiness mean to you? How does it feel? Where is the source?

Bringing happiness to life in this way is like the sun shining its rays on a seedling; it is very nourishing.

WHAT MAKES YOU FEEL CONNECTED?

Make a list of all the types of situation, the people and things that spark a feeling of connection within you. From reading a book that fires your imagination or gathering with friends at the beach, to playing catch with a dog or walking through the trees. It may be obvious to say this, but unless we consciously acknowledge moments of connection, we will take them for granted and miss the opportunity to shape our lives so that we can feel more connection.

Feeling connected is an incredible source of grounding energy – it is extremely nourishing to our sense of self. So, take a few minutes to bathe in that energy as you list anything that helps you to feel connected, whether great or small. These moments give you an appreciation of life as it is, rather than as you feel it should be.

WHAT OR WHO DO YOU NEED TO FORGIVE?

If seeing this question triggers a painful response, take your time and come back to the question when you feel able. For the moment, bring your awareness to the feelings that have been triggered, and if you wish to write anything down, then do so.

It is a good idea to practise with small acts of forgiveness – little grievances that in the great scheme of things don't matter, especially in this present moment. Writing down your forgiveness is a powerful act; notice your emotions and what is happening in your body as you put pen to paper. You might feel a sense of relief or release, or you might feel that you're not sure you mean it, you're not ready. There is no pressure to forgive in this moment, no pressure to force your feelings; simply accept and acknowledge whatever feelings arise, fully in the moment.

Do you have the sense that perhaps you need to forgive yourself? You might not even know exactly why or what for, but you carry old remnants of guilt around with you. Ask yourself: where do you feel this guilt in your body in this moment? Breathe into that place and the sensation you find there. Imagine breathing compassion into this place and simply sit in awareness, observing but not attaching to any thoughts and feelings that come…and go.

There is no need to resolve this question in this moment, but allow yourself to inquire into the thoughts and feelings that arise when it is posed.

WHAT IS GETTING
IN THE WAY?

Are there any places in your life where you feel there is a sticking point, or a block of some kind, between where you are right now and where you wish to be?

The first part of this exercise is to ask yourself this question today and not to censor the answers that come.

Once you have identified the blocks, then begin to explore whether you have positioned them as external forces that you feel are beyond your control. Imagine the same block or obstacle, but bring it within yourself; you are no longer powerless. Imagine how you might go around the obstacle or release its power over you, even for these few minutes. What choices would you need to make?

Often blocks are of our own making, and we might realize this when we give ourselves some time and space to consider where in our life we feel a little stuck. Old habits and patterns have incredible strength over our behaviours and thoughts, they are a well-worn groove. Is there an old limiting belief that you have about yourself, which it might be time to question?

IF MONEY WERE NO OBJECT, WHAT WOULD YOU DO?

It is completely normal to feel constrained by circumstances such as how much money we earn. There is a human tendency, for most (if not all) of us, to focus on where there is something missing in our lives, such as a certain amount of money or a certain type of love. The irony is that by putting our awareness onto the lack, we simply strengthen its hold over us.

Before you begin to write, take time to bring your awareness to yourself and your breath. Your thoughts will continue to come, but allow them to come and then go; there's no need to attach yourself to any of them as they drift in and out of focus.

When you can sense your presence, simply ask yourself to imagine what you would do if money were no object. Observe what comes up and then describe the scene in as much detail as you are able to. If your answer is "I don't know", that's absolutely okay, too. Be present to the "not knowing", sit with it and stay present, observing any thoughts and feelings that arise.

MINDFUL MANIFESTATION

"Everything rests on the tip of intention."

TIBETAN PROVERB

This exercise practises the power of intention. Intention is like a seed, it is the commitment and the determination to act in a certain way, but it doesn't rely on any attachment to a specific outcome. After all, you cannot control the future, only how you act in this moment.

Now that you are building your awareness to your own presence and the presence of the world around you, your intentions will become clearer; they will speak to you from within. As you write in your journal today, simply listen out for your inner voice of intention and write down what you hear, feel or see. How do you wish your life to manifest itself? Be present to all your senses.

YOUR DREAMS WILL HELP YOU

A funny thing happens when you begin to write down your dreams on waking; you begin to remember your dreams more and more. Our dreams give us access to our vast unconsciousness; and one of the most effective ways to allow our dreams to help us in our waking lives is simply to ask questions and write down whatever comes.

What felt like the most significant part of the dream?

Was there anything that felt like it was a symbol? How would you describe the characteristics of that thing, and does it relate to something or someone in your life?

How do you feel about the dream?

"*Dreams are the most curious asides and soliloquies of the soul. When a man recollects his dream, it is like meeting the ghost of himself. Dreams often surprise us into the strangest self-knowledge…*"

ALEXANDER SMITH, "ON DREAMS AND DREAMING"

MINDFUL MOMENTS

Mindfulness is in the moments, and the following prompts and exercises bring you into the detail of the moments in your life. The act of describing and writing down experiences encourages us to pay more attention generally. It sharpens our powers of observation, so that we might look up at the exact moment a beautiful bird flies overhead or absorb the joy in the laughter of a toddler nearby.

A SENSE OF AWE

"Though we travel the world over to find the beautiful, we must carry it with us or we find it not."

RALPH WALDO EMERSON

According to researchers, the experience of "awe" – that sense when a piece of art or music, or a view in nature, stops you in your tracks and moves you – is very good for your mental health. In traditional Japanese aesthetics, the concept of "yugen" means "a profound, mysterious sense of the beauty of the universe", and there really are moments that either take our breath away or are "mind-blowing".

When have you experienced a sense of awe?

COMPLETE RELAXATION

In today's world, relaxation is an essential tonic that brings the mind and body back into balance. Laying down your "busyness" is not only good for you, but for everyone around you, as you are able to recharge your batteries and just *be* for a little while, with no pressure to do anything.

When do you feel utterly relaxed? Having a massage? Listening to music? Being transported to another world by a book? Pushing your body to its limits?

Bathe in those feelings of relaxation and find time to bring relaxation into your life. Your mind will thank you.

Make a list of everything that helps you to feel relaxed.

THE NIGHT SKY

Gaze at this image or at the actual night sky tonight.

What do you think about?

What do you feel?

Let your imagination go out into the universe and explore.

THE DEER IN THE FOREST

Find a comfortable place to sit and gently bring your attention to your breath, allowing your thoughts to begin to slow down and settle. Become the observer of your thoughts as they drift in and out of your mind, like clouds across the sky.

Now, imagine that you are walking through a forest, with sunlight filtering through the leaves of the trees, the smell of the earth beneath your feet and the sounds of nature all around you. You are walking at a natural pace, noticing the details – the patterns of the bark, the signs of the season, the cool breeze on your skin.

There, ahead of you on the path, you see a beautiful doe which, at the same time, has spotted you and is looking toward you with calm curiosity. You stand completely still, relaxed but motionless, looking straight into the eyes of the doe, which are full of nature's wisdom.

Is there a question you wish to ask the doe? What question is rising up in your mind? Go ahead and ask.

Look deeply into the doe's eyes...relax and wait for the answer.

"We hear only those questions for which we are in a position to find answers."

FRIEDRICH NIETZSCHE

AN EVERYDAY MOMENT

"Can washing up really be good for you? Can we discover a moment of insight, a wave of calm, a tickle of delight or a tingle of connection within our simple, readily available, everyday routine?"

THE DEPARTMENT STORE FOR THE MIND,
WASHING UP IS GOOD FOR YOU

Describe an activity or a moment that occurs every day, which always catches your attention. It might be the warm feeling of walking through your front door at the end of the day, or walking past that lovely garden on the way to the bus. It might be as simple as splashing your face with water, or making a cup of tea. The seemingly small things really do have an impact, especially when we bring our awareness to them.

SEEING PATTERNS

The following prompts and exercises are offered as a way of bringing your awareness and attention to the patterns in your life – the stunning patterns in nature that perhaps reflect your mind's ability to create webs and well-worn paths that seem to go around and around!

THE PATTERNS
AROUND YOU

The world, whether natural or man-made, is full of fascinating patterns. Even some vegetables have the most extraordinary geometrical patterns when you slice them open, like the humble red cabbage. The tide leaves the most beautiful curved patterns on a sandy beach, while each and every snowflake is a unique, crystal-like structure. A spiral staircase creates a pattern of opportunity as one looks up, while shelves full of books signal potential and so much creativity.

What patterns can you see around you?

CLOUDS
IN THE SKY

"Clouds come floating into my life, no longer to carry rain or usher storm, but to add colour to my sunset sky."

RABINDRANATH TAGORE

Clouds remind us to stop looking down at our feet and instead look up to the sky. The patterns and shapes they create are awe-inspiring, and connect us immediately with the world, the weather and the atmosphere. Wispy cirrus clouds, big cotton-wool cumulus clouds that seem all shades of pristine white. Storm clouds that suddenly transform a blue-sky day into darkness.

And like our thoughts, clouds are impermanent, for no cloud stays the same as it travels across the sky. And just like that, they disappear.

What can you see in the clouds today?

WHAT'S YOUR STORY?

Now that you are in the swing of noticing patterns, this is an invitation to look at the patterns in your life and in your behaviour, the old repetitive (and usually limiting) ways in which you describe yourself or the characteristics you identify with.

Lines that might start with:

I always…

I never…

I can't…

I won't…

How would you fill in the blanks?

WHAT'S THE PAY-OFF?

Take something about yourself or a behaviour pattern that you would like to change. It can be very frustrating when we know we want to change, but we keep ending up on the same merry-go-round over and over again. It might be wanting to eat more healthily or spend more time outside the office, or we might wish to be more optimistic, but find that pessimism is such an ingrained trait that we find ourselves walking down that path without even realizing it.

If you bring your mindful awareness to the thing that you wish to change, consider what is the pay-off for not changing, for continuing as you are, however unhelpful the behaviour. This exploration allows you to go right to the heart of the behaviour, back to when it was useful in some way. Perhaps it keeps you in your comfort zone; perhaps change is actually quite daunting and fraught with the risk that you might fail.

Take a few minutes now to express the reasons why you would not change. Feel whether these reasons are your truth or whether they are, just possibly, the excuses you give yourself not to take a chance.

EVIDENCE TO THE CONTRARY

"Yesterday I was clever, so I wanted to change the world. Today I am wise, so I am changing myself."

RUMI

It's easy to become very attached to a fixed sense of identity, when in reality we can change at any given moment, if we are willing to let go. If you feel you aren't a very courageous, creative or generous person, you can be any of those things, and you have been all of those things.

Today is the day to stop building up the piles of evidence that support any kind of fixed ideas you have about yourself, or others. Today, look for evidence to the contrary and write it down.

GRATITUDE FOR WHAT IS

There have been many studies which have found
that practising and developing gratitude are good
for both our mental and physical health. Researchers
at Northeastern University, Boston, MA, found that
people who consciously felt a sense of gratitude each
day became more patient and found it easier to make
decisions. Other studies have discovered that feelings
of gratitude are linked to healthy habits such as
exercising and eating well. And it might be obvious to
say it, but gratitude is beneficial to our relationships
and the way we feel about life in general, boosting
feelings of happiness, love and wellbeing.

FIVE MINUTES
OF GRATITUDE

For this mindful writing exercise, which you can repeat at any time, all you have to do is let your mind and your heart run free, as you list everything you can think of in this moment that you are grateful for. You might be surprised by just how many things you can write down in a five minutes. There are no rules – absolutely anything or anyone can be included.

A THANK-YOU NOTE

"Let us be grateful to the people who make us happy; they are the charming gardeners who make our souls blossom."

MARCEL PROUST

You might be familiar with writing thank-you notes for presents or if you've been invited around to dinner, but for this exercise you don't have to worry about the other person reading your letter and so you can really speak from the heart.

What is it about another person that you are grateful for? Is it their actions, which you might describe, or their behaviour? What qualities do you admire in them? Is there something specific they have done for you, or is it because you know they are there for you?

It doesn't matter how you word your note, let your gratitude for this person flow.

THE WEATHER

Like the clouds in the sky, weather in general is never permanent or fixed. Sometimes we find ourselves grumbling about the rain or the cold, but for now, in this moment, describe your favourite kind of weather in as much detail as you can. How does it make you feel? What are the smells that you associate with this weather, the memories, the activities? Why do you love it so much?

"Sunshine is delicious, rain is refreshing, wind braces us up, snow is exhilarating; there is really no such thing as bad weather, only different kinds of good weather."

JOHN RUSKIN

A PLACE TO SIT

You might be sitting in this place right now, or you can easily imagine a favourite sitting spot, whether at home, out in nature or in a gallery or museum.

Describe the place and why you like to sit there – what does it evoke for you? Is it deeply relaxing, inspiring, or that place where you can just switch off? Perhaps, like Virginia Woolf, it is a room of your own, or a flat rock at the beach; or a perfectly cut tree stump.

ART TO BE THANKFUL FOR

Art – whether in the form of a book, a painting, music, theatre, film or any other expression of creativity – has a way of bringing us into the moment, into the experience of the present. Perhaps that it why it is so essential to life, even though it doesn't give us food, water or shelter.

What expression of creativity has recently made an impression on you?

"The main thing is to be moved, to love, to hope, to tremble, to live."

AUGUSTE RODIN

THANKS TO NATURE

When you give your attention to nature, it will repay you a thousand times over with details full of wonder. The sheer amount of life that can be sensed in nature at any moment is one of the most visceral reminders of presence. The birds aren't worried about where the next worm is going to come from, they are just out there finding them.

Nature stimulates all of our senses and reminds us of where we are.
What are you thankful to nature for today?

_____

_____

_____

_____

_____

_____

_____

_____

_____

_____

_____

_____

_____

_____

_____

A WONDERFUL
TIME OF THE DAY

Describe for a few minutes a time of the day that you appreciate.
What is it about that time of day that stands out, and what feelings are
associated with it? Is it a time full of potential, or perhaps a time filled
with peace or the joy of being with others?

Each day the sun rises and sets, reminding us that nothing is permanent,
that time can never stand still. But with our awareness we bring richness
in detail and colour to the experience of each day, from the moment we
awake to the moment we drift into sleep.

A LOVELY TIME
OF THE YEAR

Sometimes we find ourselves aching for the signs of spring after a long winter, but during the winter we have the chance to come in from the cold into a warm kitchen or to feel renewed by the chill on our cheeks. We dance in the summer, and then begin to settle again as autumn comes with all its mists and fruitfulness.

Like all the entries in this journal, today you might describe a day in winter, and tomorrow spring. But at this moment feel the seasons where you live, which might be pronounced or very nuanced, and describe a favourite time.

"The seasons and all their changes are in me."

HENRY DAVID THOREAU

HOW COULD YOU SHOW YOUR GRATITUDE?

If you consider that long list of people and things that you are grateful for, take a few minutes to write mindfully now about how you might show your gratitude in your own way. Perhaps you might wish to say thank you to the environment around you by consciously using less plastic, or you might thank a loved one by calling them at the weekend, as they always love to have a chat. You might suggest meeting up with an old friend, or simply tell someone that you are thinking of them in this moment.

How would you like to show your gratitude today?

_____

_____

_____

_____

_____

_____

_____

_____

_____

_____

_____

_____

_____

_____

_____

_____

WHAT DOES KINDNESS MEAN TO YOU?

"No act of kindness, however small, is wasted."

AESOP

Just by describing kindness, you will notice it more easily when it shows up, in the smallest to the biggest acts, words or thoughts. Whenever you bring awareness to something, it magically appears.

HOW CAN YOU BE KINDER TO YOURSELF?

Like any expression of love, kindness is much easier to share with others when you are willing to give it to yourself, to treat yourself as you would a dear friend.

It is often easier to be self-critical or look for our flaws than it is to be compassionate and loving toward ourselves. But the key to loving others begins when we learn to love ourselves, just as we are.

How can you be kinder to yourself today? Is it with the gift of time for meditation or quiet contemplation, the gift of delicious healthy food eaten mindfully, a phone call with a loved one? Can you put aside the self-critic and celebrate your daily accomplishments?

HOW CAN YOU DEVELOP YOUR KINDNESS TO OTHERS?

Sometimes it is easy to be kind; it comes very naturally. At other times, judgments or our own problems can get in the way of our kindness. That's natural, too. But if we become more aware of our kindness, then it will blossom, reaching into those pockets of judgment or frustration. And if we are willing to become more aware of our lack of kindness, without being self-critical or loading ourselves up with guilt, we also have the chance to dig out a few weeds.

*"Kindness is a language which the deaf
can hear and the blind can see."*

MARK TWAIN

WRITING PROMPTS
FOR MINDFULNESS

The following entries are prompts that you might
wish to return to as you develop your mindful writing
practice, along with any others that have particularly
resonated with you or are gently asking for further
exploration and inquiry.

LET GO OF THE DAY

"Be like a tree and let the dead leaves drop."

RUMI

If you're not careful, it's easy to find yourself carrying a great deal of emotional and mental baggage around with you throughout the day: old stories, hurts, patterns of behaviour, self-beliefs and preconceptions about others. No wonder you feel laden down. As you write, imagine putting all these bags down and sensing how much lighter and freer you feel.

What can you let go of today?

WHAT ARE YOUR WORDS TO LIVE BY?

These words are not static or to be followed in a rigid fashion, and might change as life unfolds, but now that you have got to know yourself with a sense of awareness, observation and inquiry, your values will be clearer and may be helpful as you live in a more mindful way.

Here are some examples of values that might speak to you, but there are many more, so listen to your heart and put down the words you presently wish to live by.

Achievement	Enjoyment	Justice
Ambition	Excellence	Kindess
Awareness	Expertise	Loyalty
Balance	Exploration	Love
Beauty	Family	Passion
Carefulness	Fearlessness	Potential
Collaboration	Freedom	Prosperity
Community	Giving	Purpose
Connection	Growth	Recognition
Conviction	Harmony	Service
Creativity	Honesty	Spirituality
Daring	Intelligence	Trust
Dedication	Intuitiveness	Wonder

YES

"I want to know if you can live with failure, yours and mine, and still stand on the edge of the lake and shout to the silver of the full moon, 'Yes!'"

ORIAH MOUNTAIN DREAMER, *THE INVITATION*

Feel the word "Yes" and where it lands in your body.

What are the thoughts and feelings that arise?

What do you wish to say "Yes!" to?

_____

_____

_____

_____

_____

_____

_____

_____

_____

_____

_____

_____

_____

_____

_____

NO

Just as we need to listen to the whispers of our heart when it comes to saying "Yes", the same is true for knowing when we need to say "No". Your body will tell you, if you are open to reading the signs. As you become practised at listening it will come naturally, but you can begin the practice by considering the word, "No", and explore what it brings up for you. Does it make you uncomfortable to say "No", or do you find it difficult to draw boundaries? Or do you tell yourself "No" too often, out of fear or anxiety? There is immense power in this tiny word.

WHAT RESOURCES DO YOU CARRY WITH YOU TODAY?

This is a wonderful way to remind yourself that each day you step out into the world you are not alone, and that you have many resources that you can access, when needed.

Draw a stick figure representing you.

On and around your stick figure, draw or write all the resources that you have access to and that support you.

These might include:

Friends and family
A roof over your head
Healthy food
Meditation
A space where you can relax
Nature
Your work
Hobbies

You might be surprised at the treasure trove you have created.

WHAT DO I WANT TO KNOW TODAY?

"Our happiness depends on wisdom all the way."

SOPHOCLES

Inquiry and exploration lead to deeper understanding. This isn't about filling up your head with facts and figures, but is linked to that inner sense of knowing. What would you wish to know today, if you could know anything?

WHAT DO I WANT TO DO TODAY?

The aim here isn't to write a traditional "to do" list of tasks for the day, but to consider how you will align your daily actions with your bigger goals or values. In other words, it is a "to do" list written in awareness.

If you could only write one thing down for the day ahead, what would it be? What's the priority for you and your life at this time, today? Give the question consideration, rather than leaping quickly to all the "shoulds".

MINDFUL NOTES TO SELF

"Let your life lightly dance on the edges of Time like dew on the tip of a leaf."

RABINDRANATH TAGORE

Here is some space to take stock of your journaling journey so far. Which prompts resonated with you most? Which exercises would you like to take forward as you develop your mindfulness practice and continue on the path of self-reflection?

Sometimes it can be the simplest reminders that enable us to bring more awareness and attention into the moments of our lives. By describing the scent of a flower, we remind ourselves to pause long enough to notice the flowers in bloom at different times of the year. By writing a list of everything we can think of to be grateful for, we instantly draw on our own well of support and happiness.

ACKNOWLEDGMENTS

Picture credits: iStock aluxum 102-103; Andrew Howe 26; Axel Ellerhorst 154; bgfoto 14–15; blyjak 114–115; borchee 134; DNY59 67; elenaleonova 125; Everste 83; greenleaf123 146; Jeja 30–31; MarioGuti 46; mukk 90–91; Oxford 149; photographer3431 99; Rike 52-53, 131; Scacciamosche 126; STILLFX 140–141; YinYang 63; ZCLiu 22; zodebala 59; zoom-zoom 89. **Unsplash** Annie Spratt 122; Blanca Paloma Sanchez 25; Dan Grinwis 75; Evie Shaffer 9; Filip Zrnzevic 17; Gaelle Marcel 54; Jamie Street 68–69; Joao Silas 11; Matt Hoffman 38; Nathan Dumlao 19; Preben Nilsen 104; Rob Potter 13; Sergei Akulich 121; Shawnn Tan 139; Valentina Dominguez 107; Wil Stewart 97.

Acknowledgments

p. 98, Inspired by Danielle Marchant, *Pause* podcast 3 August 2017

p. 100, Copyright © Dept Limited, *Washing Up is Good for You* 2017

p. 146, "The Invitation" by Oriah "Mountain Dreamer" House is from the book of the same name. © 1999. Published by HarperONE, San Francisco. All rights reserved. Presented with permission of the author.

p. 150, Inspired by Emma Cannon, *90 Days Fertile* 2018

Consultant Publisher and words by: Kate Adams
Assistant Editor: Nell Warner
Senior Designer: Jaz Bahra
Designer & Illustrator: Ella McLean
Picture Library Manager: Jen Veall
Picture Research Manager: Giulia Hetherington
Assistant Production Manager: Lucy Carter